Raw Vegan
60 The most delic

Copyright

All rights reserved. No part of this publication can be reproduced in any form or by any means including scanning, photocopying, or otherwise without prior written permission of the copyright holder.

Description

Get ready for an amazing life changing experience!

Prepare yourself for the culinary journey of a lifetime!

"Raw Vegan Salads" is here to amaze you!

Once you start reading this cookbook, you will begin to understand and love veganism!

You will end up becoming a vegan and recommending this lifestyle to everyone around you!

"Raw Vegan Salads" is the best of its kind! There's no way you'll find something like this on the market! It's a special cooking journal meant to gain your appreciation in no time!

Trust us! It's a true cooking guide that contains the best and most delicious vegan salad recipes!

Just check them out and enjoy!

Introduction

It's time for some changes in your life! It's time to become a healthier and happier person! It's time for veganism!

Don't worry! You don't need to deprive yourself or to make complex changes! You just have to give up eating processed foods, meat, fish, eggs or anything that comes from animal sources!

We can assure you that it's not hard at all!

It will soon become your new lifestyle and you will end up recommending it to others!

You will feel good, you will look good and you will even get rid of some of the extra weight that's bothering you!

In order to help you get started with this new life experience, we gathered some of the most delicious vegan salads just for you!

We bring to you some beautiful, colored, textured and flavored vegan salads!

We are sure you will love each and every one of these next salads because they can impress even the most pretentious people!

So, let's not wait too long and get to the fun part!

Have the time of your life with this special cookbook and surprise everyone with these next salads!

Enjoy!

The Most Amazing Vegan Salads Recipes

Incredible Kale Salad And Delicious Dressing

You've got to try this nutritious salad as soon as possible!

Preparation time: 10 minutes
Cooking time: 0 minutes
Servings: 4
Ingredients:
8 cups kale leaves, roughly chopped
A pinch of sea salt
Black pepper to the taste
1 tablespoon olive oil
Juice from ½ lemon
1 avocado, pitted, peeled and chopped
15 ounces canned garbanzo beans, drained
1/3 cup almonds, chopped
¼ cup red onion, chopped
1/3 cup cranberries, dried
For the salad dressing:
6 tablespoons water
½ cup tahini paste
Juice from 1 lemon
A pinch of sea salt
Directions:

In a bowl, mix tahini with juice from 1 lemon and a pinch of salt and whisk well.

In a large salad bowl, mix kale with avocado, onion, beans, cranberries and almonds.

Add juice from ½ lemon, 1 tablespoon oil, a pinch of salt and black pepper and toss to coat.

Add the tahini salad dressing, toss well and serve right away.
Enjoy!

Nutrition: calories 140, fat 2, fiber 2, carbs 5, protein 9

Pear And Pomegranate Salad

This salad is meant to impress you and your guests!

Preparation time: 10 minutes

Cooking time: 0 minutes

Servings: 3

Ingredients:

3 big Asian pears, cored and cut with a spiralizer

¾ cup pomegranate seeds

5 ounces arugula

¾ cup walnuts, roughly chopped

For the vinaigrette:

1 tablespoon sesame oil

1 tablespoon olive oil

1 tablespoon maple syrup

1 teaspoon white sesame seeds

2 tablespoons apple cider vinegar

1 tablespoon soy sauce

1 garlic clove, minced

A pinch of sea salt

Black pepper to the taste

Directions:

In a bowl, mix sesame oil with olive oil, maple syrup, sesame seeds, vinegar, garlic, soy sauce, salt and pepper and whisk very well.

In a salad bowl, mix pear noodles with arugula, walnuts and pomegranate seeds.

Add vinaigrette, toss to coat well and serve right away.

Nutrition: calories 200, fat 2, fiber 7, carbs 12, protein 9

Delicious Bulgur Salad

This is so flavored and healthy!

Preparation time: 15 minutes
Cooking time: 0 minutes
Servings: 6
Ingredients:
1 and ½ cups hot water
1 cup bulgur
Juice from 1 lime
4 tablespoons cilantro, chopped
½ cup cranberries, dried
1 lime, cut into wedges
A pinch of cumin, ground
1 and ½ teaspoons curry powder
1/3 cup almonds, sliced
¼ cup green onions, chopped
½ cup red bell peppers, chopped
½ cup carrots, grated
4 tablespoons pepitas
1 tablespoon olive oil
A pinch of sea salt
Black pepper to the taste

Directions:
Put bulgur into a bowl, add boiling water over it, stir, cover and leave aside for 15 minutes.

Fluff bulgur with a fork and transfer to a salad bowl.

Add lime juice, cilantro, cranberries, almonds, bell peppers, onions and carrots and stir.

Add cumin, curry powder and pepitas and stir again.

Add oil, a pinch of salt and black pepper, stir and serve right away with lime wedges on the side.

Enjoy!

Nutrition: calories 160, fat 3, fiber 3, carbs 7, protein 10

Amazing Black Bean Salad

This is easy to make and it tastes great!

Preparation time: 15 minutes

Cooking time: 0 minutes

Servings: 4

Ingredients:

1 and ½ cups cooked black beans
½ teaspoon garlic powder
½ teaspoon smoked paprika
2 teaspoons chili powder
A pinch of sea salt
Black pepper to the taste
1 teaspoon cumin
A pinch of cayenne pepper
1 and ½ cups chickpeas, cooked
¼ teaspoon cinnamon
1 lettuce head, chopped
1 red bell pepper, chopped
2 tomatoes, chopped
1 avocado, pitted, peeled and chopped
1 cup corn kernels, chopped

For the salad dressing:

2 tablespoons lemon juice
¾ cup cashews, soaked for a couple of hours and drained
½ cup water
1 garlic clove, minced
1 tablespoon apple cider vinegar
½ teaspoon onion powder
1 teaspoon chives, chopped
½ teaspoon oregano, dried
1 teaspoon dill, dried
1 teaspoon cumin
½ teaspoon smoked paprika

Directions:

In your blender, mix cashews with water, 2 tablespoons lemon juice, 1 tablespoon vinegar, 1 garlic clove, ½ teaspoon onion powder, dill, oregano, chives, 1 teaspoon cumin, a pinch of salt and ½ teaspoon paprika, blend really well and leave aside for now.

In a salad bowl, mix black beans with chili powder, ½ teaspoon garlic powder, ½ teaspoon paprika, 1 teaspoon cumin, cayenne, chickpeas, cinnamon, a pinch of salt and black pepper to the taste and stir really well.

Add lettuce leaves, tomatoes, corn, avocado and bell peppers and stir everything.

Drizzle the salad dressing all over your salad, toss to coat and serve right away. Enjoy!

Nutrition: calories 300, fat 4, fiber 10, carbs 16, protein 18

Great Cucumber Salad

This is the best way to end a stressful day!

Preparation time: 15 minutes

Cooking time: 0 minutes

Servings: 4

Ingredients:

3 big cucumbers, sliced

1 tablespoon sesame oil

A pinch of sea salt

Black pepper to the taste

3 green onions, chopped

3 carrots, shaved

½ cup cilantro, chopped

1 red chili pepper, chopped

1 small green bell pepper, chopped

1/3 cup almonds, chopped

For the salad dressing:

3 tablespoons sesame oil

2 garlic cloves, minced

1 small ginger piece, grated

1 tablespoon soy sauce

2 tablespoons rice vinegar

1 teaspoon maple syrup

A pinch of red pepper flakes

Directions:

In a bowl, whisk sesame oil with garlic, ginger, soy sauce, vinegar, maple syrup and pepper flakes and whisk well.

In a salad bowl, mix cucumbers with onions, cilantro, carrots, chili pepper, green bell pepper and almonds and stir.

Add 1 tablespoon sesame oil, a pinch of salt and some black pepper and stir.

Add salad dressing, toss to coat and serve.

Enjoy!

Nutrition: calories 120, fat 3, fiber 2, carbs 4, protein 10

Zucchini Noodles Salad

The combination of ingredients is really great!

Preparation time: 30 minutes
Cooking time: 0 minutes
Servings: 4
Ingredients:
2 zucchinis, cut with a spiralizer
1 cup pickled beets
½ bunch kale, chopped
2 tablespoons sesame oil
2 teaspoons tamari
1 tablespoon liquid smoke
14 ounces tofu, drained and cut in medium pieces
For the tahini sauce:
1 tablespoon maple syrup
Juice from 1 lemon
¼ inch ginger, grated
1/3 cup tahini paste

Directions:

Put tofu in a bowl, add liquid smoke, tamari and sesame oil, toss to coat and leave aside for 20 minutes.

Put tofu pieces in your waffle iron, cook according to instructions and leave aside for now.

In another bowl, mix lemon juice with maple syrup, ginger and tahini paste and whisk well.

In a salad bowl, mix zucchini noodles with beets, kale and tofu.

Add tahini sauce, toss to coat and serve right away.

Enjoy!

Nutrition: calories 200, fat 3, fiber 2, carbs 7, protein 19

Delicious Lentils Salad

This is so refreshing and delicious!

Preparation time: 10 minutes

Cooking time: 0 minutes

Servings: 2

Ingredients:

1 pita bread, cubed

1/3 cup canned and cooked green lentils, drained

2 teaspoons olive oil

1 carrot, grated

4 cups arugula

2 celery stalks, chopped

1 cucumber, sliced

¼ cup dates, pitted and chopped

1 radish, sliced

2 tablespoons sunflower seeds

For the vinaigrette:

1 tablespoon maple syrup

1 tablespoon Dijon mustard

2 tablespoons balsamic vinegar

2 tablespoons olive oil

Directions:

In a bowl, mix maple syrup with mustard, vinegar and olive oil and whisk well.

In a salad bowl, mix green lentils with bread cubes, carrot, arugula, celery, cucumber, dates, radish and sunflower seeds.

Add 2 teaspoons oil and toss to coat.

Add the vinaigrette you've made, toss again and serve.

Enjoy!

Nutrition: calories 179, fat 4, fiber 3, carbs 8, protein 12

Chickpeas And Spinach Salad

How can you not love this salad?

Preparation time: 15 minutes
Cooking time: 0 minutes
Servings: 2
Ingredients:
16 ounces canned chickpeas, drained
1 handful raisins
1 handful baby spinach leaves
1 tablespoon maple syrup
½ tablespoon lemon juice
4 tablespoons olive oil
1 teaspoon cumin, ground
A pinch of sea salt
Black pepper to the taste
½ teaspoon chili flakes

Directions:

In a bowl, mix maple syrup with lemon juice, oil, cumin, a pinch of salt, black pepper and chili flakes and whisk well.

In a salad bowl, mix chickpeas with spinach and raisins and stir.

Add salad dressing, toss to coat and serve.

Enjoy!

Nutrition: calories 300, fat 3, fiber 6, carbs 12, protein 9

Easy Carrots Slaw

This is very easy and delicious! You can make it at home tonight!

Preparation time: 10 minutes
Cooking time: 0 minutes
Servings: 4
Ingredients:
1 and ½ tablespoon maple syrup
1 teaspoon coconut oil, melted
3 teaspoons tamari sauce
1 tablespoon walnuts, chopped
1 onion, chopped
4 cups carrots, shredded
1 tablespoon curry powder
¼ teaspoon turmeric powder
Black pepper to the taste
2 tablespoons tahini paste
¼ cup lemon juice
½ cup parsley, chopped
A pinch of cayenne pepper

Directions:
In a bowl, mix carrots with walnuts and onion and stir.
Add maple syrup, coconut oil and tamari and stir well.
Also add curry powder, turmeric, black pepper, tahini, lemon juice, cayenne and the parsley, toss well and keep in the fridge until you serve.
Enjoy!
Nutrition: calories 150, fat 3, fiber 2, carbs 6, protein 10

Delicious Greek Salad

Try a tasty Mediterranean salad tonight!

Preparation time: 10 minutes
Cooking time: 0 minutes
Servings: 4
Ingredients:
1 handful kalamata olives, pitted and sliced
1 punnet cherry tomatoes, halved
4 tomatoes, chopped
1 and ½ cucumbers, sliced
1 red onion, chopped
2 tablespoons oregano, chopped
1 tablespoon mint, chopped
For the salad dressing:
1 teaspoon coconut sugar
2 tablespoons balsamic vinegar
¼ cup olive oil
1 garlic clove, minced
2 teaspoons Italian herbs, dried
1 teaspoon soy sauce
A pinch of sea salt
Black pepper to the taste

Directions:

In a salad bowl, mix cherry tomatoes with tomatoes, olives, cucumbers, onion, mint and oregano and stir.

In another bowl, mix sugar with vinegar, oil, garlic, dried Italian herbs, soy sauce, a pinch of salt and black pepper and whisk well.

Add this to salad, toss to coat and serve.

Enjoy!

Nutrition: calories 140, fat 2, fiber 3, carbs 6, protein 12

Super Fast Salad

How can you not love this salad?

Preparation time: 10 minutes

Cooking time: 0 minutes

Servings: 4

Ingredients:

15 ounces canned chickpeas, drained

15 ounces canned great northern beans, drained

2 tablespoons olive oil

½ cup spinach, chopped

½ cup cucumber, sliced

1 tablespoon basil, chopped

1 tablespoon parsley, chopped

8 sun dried tomatoes, chopped

A pinch of sea salt

2 tablespoon vinegar

Directions:

In a bowl, mix chickpeas with beans, spinach, cucumber, tomatoes, basil and parsley.

Add salt, vinegar and oil, toss to coat well and serve.

Enjoy!

Nutrition: calories 140, fat 5, fiber 6, carbs 9, protein 15

Amazing Avocado And Beans Salad

It's rich and textured! You should try this salad soon!

Preparation time: 10 minutes

Cooking time: 0 minutes

Servings: 4

Ingredients:

15 ounces canned white beans, drained
1 tomato, chopped
1 avocado, pitted, peeled and chopped
¼ sweet onion, chopped
A pinch of sea salt
Black pepper to the taste
¼ cup lemon juice
1 and ½ tablespoons olive oil
A handful basil, chopped
1 teaspoon garlic, minced
1 teaspoon mustard

Directions:

In a salad bowl, mix beans with tomato, avocado and onion.
Add a pinch of salt and black pepper and stir gently everything.
In a bowl, mix oil with lemon juice, basil, mustard and garlic and whisk well.
Add this to the salad, toss to coat and serve.
Enjoy!

Nutrition: calories 150, fat 3, fiber 2, carbs 6, protein 14

Incredible Thai Salad

Find out what you need in order to make this special salad!

Preparation time: 10 minutes
Cooking time: 0 minutes
Servings: 4
Ingredients:
2 zucchinis, cut with a veggie peeler
2 cups bean sprouts
4 green onions, chopped
1 red bell pepper, chopped
Juice from 1 lime
1 tablespoon olive oil
½ cup cilantro, chopped
¾ cup almonds, chopped
A pinch of sea salt
Black pepper to the taste
Directions:
In a salad bowl, mix zucchinis with bean sprouts, onions and bell pepper.
Add salt, pepper, lime juice and olive oil and toss everything.
Add cilantro, stir and top with almonds.
Enjoy!
Nutrition: calories 140, fat 4, fiber 2, carbs 7, protein 12

Delicious Cabbage And Coconut Salad

Are you looking for an Indian style vegan salad? This is perfect!

Preparation time: 1 hour and 10 minutes
Cooking time: 0 minutes
Servings: 4
Ingredients:
1 green cabbage head, chopped
1/3 cup coconut, shredded
¼ cup olive oil
2 tablespoons lemon juice
¼ cup soy sauce
3 tablespoons sesame seeds
½ teaspoon curry powder
1/3 teaspoon turmeric
½ teaspoon cumin

Directions:
In a bowl, mix cabbage with coconut and lemon juice and stir.
Add oil, soy sauce, sesame seeds, curry powder, turmeric and cumin, toss to coat and serve after 1 hour.
Enjoy!
Nutrition: calories 130, fat 4, fiber 5, carbs 8, protein 10

Wonderful Papaya Salad

This is the best summer salad you could ever taste!

Preparation time: 10 minutes
Cooking time: 0 minutes
Servings: 4
Ingredients:
2 cups green papaya, grated
¼ cup carrots, grated
¼ cup green beans, chopped
2 tablespoons soy sauce
¼ cup cabbage, shredded
10 cherry tomatoes, halved
2 Thai chilies, chopped
2 garlic cloves, minced
1 teaspoon lemon juice
1 teaspoon agave nectar
2 tablespoons peanuts, chopped
A pinch of sea salt
Black pepper to the taste
Some lettuce leaves, chopped

Directions:

In a salad bowl, mix papaya with carrots, green beans, cabbage, lettuce leaves, tomatoes, chilies and garlic.

Add soy sauce, lemon juice, agave nectar, a pinch of salt, black pepper and peanuts and stir everything.

Serve right away!

Nutrition: calories 140, fat 3, fiber 2, carbs 6, protein 8

Incredible Dinner Salad

This is what you need tonight to feel full and satisfied!

Preparation time: 1 hour and 10 minutes
Cooking time: 0 minutes
Servings: 4
Ingredients:
1 cup cabbage, shredded
1 apple, cored and chopped
1 celery rib, chopped
1 carrot, grated
4 dates, chopped
¼ cup cashews
For the salad dressing:
1 tablespoon lemon juice
2 garlic cloves, minced
¼ cup tahini paste
1 tablespoon apple cider vinegar
1 tablespoon agave nectar
2 tablespoons water
3 tablespoons olive oil
1 tablespoon parsley, chopped
A pinch of sea salt

Directions:

In a blender, mix lemon juice with garlic, tahini paste, vinegar, agave nectar, water, olive oil, parsley and a pinch of salt and blend well.

In a salad bowl, mix cabbage with celery, apple, carrots, dates and cashews and stir.

Add salad dressing, toss to coat and serve.

Enjoy!

Nutrition: calories 140, fat 3, fiber 4, carbs 5, protein 14

Corn And Avocado Salad

It's a great combination!

Preparation time: 10 minutes
Cooking time: 0 minutes
Servings: 4
Ingredients:
2 avocados, pitted, peeled and cubed
1 pint mixed cherry tomatoes, halved
2 cups fresh corn
1 red onion, chopped
For the salad dressing:
2 tablespoons olive oil
1 tablespoon lime juice
½ teaspoon lime zest, grated
A pinch of salt
Black pepper to the taste
¼ cup cilantro, chopped
Directions:
In a salad bowl, mix avocados with onion, corn and tomatoes.

In a smaller bowl, mix oil with lime juice and zest, a pinch of salt and some black pepper and whisk well.

Add this over salad, sprinkle cilantro on top, toss to coat and serve.

Nutrition: calories 120, fat 3, fiber 2, carbs 6, protein 9

Special Edamame Salad

It's different and it's special!

Preparation time: 15 minutes

Cooking time: 0 minutes

Servings: 4

Ingredients:

1 tablespoon ginger, grated

2 green onions, chopped

3 cups edamame

½ cup seaweed, dried

2 tablespoons rice vinegar

2 tablespoons tamari sauce

2 tablespoons maple syrup

1 tablespoon sesame seeds

Directions :

Put edamame in boiling water for 3 minutes and drain.

Put seaweed in a bowl, add water to cover, leave aside for 15 minutes, drain and mix with edamame.

In another bowl, mix ginger with green onion, vinegar, tamari sauce, maple syrup and sesame seeds and whisk well.

Drizzle this over salad, toss to coat and serve.

Enjoy!

Nutrition: calories 120, fat 3, fiber 2, carbs 5, protein 9

Colored Beets Salad

It's a colored and flavored salad you can try today!

Preparation time: 10 minutes
Cooking time: 0 minutes
Servings: 4
Ingredients:
4 carrots, sliced
12 radishes, sliced
1 beet, peeled and grated
2 tablespoons raisins
Juice from 2 lemons
1 sugar beet, peeled and chopped
1 tablespoon chives, chopped
1 tablespoon parsley, chopped
1 tablespoon lemon thyme, chopped
1 tablespoon white sesame seeds
4 handfuls spinach leaves
4 tablespoons linseed oil
A pinch of sea salt
Black pepper to the taste
Pansies for serving
Marigolds for serving

Directions:

In a salad bowl, mix carrots, radishes, beets, sugar beet, raisins, chives, parsley, spinach, thyme and sesame seeds.

Add lemon juice, oil, a pinch of salt and black pepper and toss well.

Add pansies and marigolds on top and serve.

Enjoy!

Nutrition: calories 110, fat 2, fiber 2, carbs 4, protein 7

Sauerkraut Salad

Why don't you try this great salad?

Preparation time: 10 minutes

Cooking time: 0 minutes

Servings: 4

Ingredients:

25 ounces sauerkraut, chopped

1 onion, chopped

1 cup walnuts, chopped

½ tablespoon cumin

1 carrot, grated

1 apple, cored and chopped

1 tablespoon mustard

1 tablespoon apple cider vinegar

1 tablespoons raisins

Directions:

In a salad bowl, mix sauerkraut with onion, walnuts, carrot, apple and cumin and stir.

Add mustard, vinegar and raisins, stir well and serve.

Enjoy!

Nutrition: calories 120, fat 1, fiber 2, carbs 2, protein 8

Delicious Summer Salad

It's going to be the best vegan salad ever and it's going to be ready in no time!

Preparation time: 10 minutes
Cooking time: 0 minutes
Servings: 6
Ingredients:
½ cup extra virgin olive oil
1 cucumber, chopped
2 pints colored cherry tomatoes, halved
Salt and black pepper to the taste
1 red onion, chopped
3 tablespoons red wine vinegar
1 garlic clove, minced
1 bunch basil, roughly chopped
1 teaspoon maple syrup
Directions:
In a bowl, mix vinegar with salt, pepper, maple syrup and oil and whisk very well.
In a salad bowl mix cucumber with tomatoes, onion and garlic.
Add vinegar dressing, toss to coat, sprinkle basil, toss to coat and serve.
Enjoy!
Nutrition: calories 100, fat 1, fiber 2, carbs 2, protein 8

Simple Tomato And Avocado Salad

It's an excellent vegan choice for a light lunch or even dinner!

Preparation time: 10 minutes

Cooking time: 0 minutes

Servings: 4

Ingredients:

1 cucumber, chopped

1 pound tomatoes, chopped

2 avocados, pitted and chopped

1 small red onion, thinly sliced

2 tablespoons olive oil

2 tablespoons lemon juice

¼ cup cilantro, finely chopped

Sea salt and black pepper to the taste

Directions:

In a salad bowl, mix tomatoes with onion, avocado, cucumber and cilantro.

In a small bowl, mix oil with lemon juice, salt and pepper to the taste and whisk well.

Pour this over salad, toss to coat and serve right away.

Enjoy!

Nutrition: calories 120, fat 2, fiber 2, carbs 3, protein 4

Amazing Tomato And Watermelon Salad

It's a fresh and juicy summer salad and it's 100% vegan!

Preparation time: 10 minutes

Cooking time: 0 minutes

Servings: 4

Ingredients:

½ teaspoon agave nectar

2 tablespoons lemon juice

1 tablespoon extra virgin olive oil

8 ounces tomatoes, chopped

1 jalapeno, seeded and chopped

12 ounces watermelon, chopped

1 red onion, thinly sliced

Salt and black pepper to the taste

½ cup basil leaves, chopped

2 cups baby arugula

Directions:

In a bowl, mix lemon juice with oil, salt, pepper and agave nectar and whisk well.

Add onion, jalapeno and tomatoes and toss to coat.

Add basil, watermelon and arugula, stir gently and serve.

Enjoy!

Nutrition: calories 100, fat 0.2, fiber 1, carbs 1, protein 8

Mediterranean Tomato Salad

It's colored, it's tasty and it's easy to make!

Preparation time: 10 minutes

Cooking time: 0 minutes

Servings: 4

Ingredients:

4 pounds heirloom tomatoes, thinly sliced
1 yellow bell pepper, thinly sliced
1 green bell pepper, thinly sliced
1 red onion, thinly sliced
Sea salt and black pepper to the taste
½ teaspoon oregano, dried
2 tablespoons mint leaves, chopped
A drizzle of extra virgin olive oil

Directions:

In a salad bowl, mix tomatoes with yellow and green peppers, onion, salt and pepper, toss to coat and leave aside for 10 minutes.

Add oregano, mint and olive oil and toss to coat.

Serve right away.

Enjoy!

Nutrition: calories 100, fat 2, fiber 2, carbs 3, protein 6

Cucumber And Dates Salad

This is a very healthy salad! Try it and enjoy its taste!

Preparation time: 10 minutes

Cooking time: 0 minutes

Servings: 4

Ingredients:

2 English cucumbers, chopped

8 dates, pitted and sliced

¾ cup fennel, thinly sliced

2 tablespoons chives, finely chopped

½ cup walnuts, chopped

2 tablespoons lemon juice

4 tablespoons fruity olive oil

Salt and black pepper to the taste

Directions:

Place cucumber pieces on a paper towel, press well and transfer to a salad bowl. Crush them a bit using a fork.

Add dates, fennel, chives and walnuts and stir gently.

Add salt, pepper to the taste, lemon juice and the oil, toss to coat and serve right away.

Enjoy!

Nutrition: calories 100, fat 1, fiber 1, carbs 1, protein 6

Cucumber And Beans Salad

You won't need anything else to eat all day!

Preparation time: 10 minutes
Cooking time: 0 minutes
Servings: 4
Ingredients:
1 big cucumber, cut in chunks
15 ounces canned black beans, drained
1 cup corn
1 cup cherry tomatoes, halved
1 small red onion, chopped
3 tablespoons olive oil
4 and ½ teaspoons vegan orange marmalade
1 teaspoon agave nectar
Salt and black pepper to the taste
½ teaspoon cumin
1 tablespoon lemon juice

Directions:
In a bowl, mix beans with cucumber, corn, onion and tomatoes.
In another bowl, mix marmalade with oil, agave nectar, lemon juice, salt, pepper to the taste and cumin and stir very well.
Pour this dressing over salad, toss to coat and serve right away.
Nutrition: calories 110, fat 0, fiber 3, carbs 6, protein 8

Fennel And Parsley Salad

You will find this really delicious!

Preparation time: 10 minutes

Cooking time: 0 minutes

Servings: 4

Ingredients:

1 tablespoon olive oil

1 teaspoon mustard

1 tablespoon lemon juice

1 fennel bulb, trimmed and shaved

Salt and black pepper to the taste

1 cup parsley, roughly chopped

Directions:

In a bowl, mix oil with mustard, lemon juice, salt and pepper and whisk very well.

In a salad bowl, mix fennel with parsley and stir.

Add the salad dressing, toss to coat and serve.

Enjoy!

Nutrition: calories 100, fat 0.5, fiber 1, carbs 1, protein 5

Tasty Grapefruit Salad

This will be a complete culinary success!

Preparation time: 10 minutes
Cooking time: 0 minutes
Servings: 4
Ingredients:
2 tablespoons lemon juice
½ teaspoon lemon zest, grated
A pinch of sea salt
Black pepper to the taste
2 teaspoons ginger, grated
½ teaspoon wasabi paste
1 tablespoon shallot, minced
1 fennel, bulb, trimmed and shaved
2 grapefruits, peeled and cut into segments
1 pear, cored and chopped
1 kiwi, peeled and roughly chopped
Directions:
In a salad bowl, mix fennel with grapefruits, pear and kiwi.

In another bowl, mix lemon juice with lemon zest, a pinch of salt, black pepper, ginger, wasabi and shallot and whisk well.

Add this to your salad, toss to coat and serve right away.
Nutrition: calories 100, fat 0, fiber 2, carbs 0, protein 5

Delicious Endives Salad

It's delicious and fresh! You should try this salad sometimes!

Preparation time: 10 minutes

Cooking time: 0 minutes

Servings: 4

Ingredients:

2 tablespoons lemon juice

¼ cup olive oil

Salt and black pepper to the taste

1 teaspoon mustard

2 fennel bulbs, trimmed and shaved

2 big endives, cut in small pieces

½ cup almonds, chopped

2 tablespoons parsley, chopped

Directions:

In a salad bowl, mix fennel with endives and almonds.

Add parsley, salt, pepper, lemon juice, oil and mustard and whisk well.

Serve right away.

Enjoy!

Nutrition: calories 100, fat 0, fiber 1, carbs 0, protein 6

Endives And Apple Salad

You must give this salad a chance! You will love it!

Preparation time: 10 minutes
Cooking time: 0 minutes
Servings: 4
Ingredients:
1 teaspoon shallot, minced
¼ cup apple cider vinegar
1 teaspoon Dijon mustard
1 teaspoon agave nectar
3 Belgian endives, cut in medium pieces
¾ cup canola oil
½ apple, cored and roughly chopped
1 cup escarole leaves, torn

Directions:
In a bowl, mix escarole leaves with endives and apple.
Add shallot, vinegar, mustard, agave nectar and oil and whisk well.
Add this to salad, toss to coat and serve.
Enjoy!

Nutrition: calories 90, fat 1, fiber 0, carbs 0, protein 7

Simple And Delicious Romaine Salad

Can you gather all the ingredients today?

Preparation time: 10 minutes

Cooking time: 0 minutes

Servings: 4

Ingredients:

½ cup olive oil

Salt and black pepper to the taste

2 tablespoons shallot, chopped

¼ cup mustard

Juice from 2 lemons

½ cup basil, chopped

5 baby romaine lettuce heads, chopped

3 radicchios, sliced

3 endives, cut in medium pieces

Directions:

In a salad bowl, mix romaine lettuce with radicchios and endives and stir gently.

In another bowl, mix oil with salt, pepper, shallot, mustard, lemon juice and basil and whisk really well.

Drizzle this over your salad, toss to coat and serve.

Enjoy!

Nutrition: calories 100, fat 2, fiber 1, carbs 1, protein 2

Delightful Radish Salad

You will adore this fresh salad once you try it!

Preparation time: 10 minutes
Cooking time: 0 minutes
Servings: 4
Ingredients:
12 ounces tomatoes, chopped
1 cucumber, chopped
3 red onions, chopped
7 ounces red radishes, cut in wedges
3 tablespoons olive oil
1 teaspoon mustard
1 teaspoon mustard seeds
Juice from 2 limes
2 teaspoons agave nectar
3 tablespoons mint, chopped
1 red chili pepper, chopped

Directions:
In a salad bowl, mix tomatoes with cucumber, onions and radishes and stir.

In another bowl, mix mustard with mustard seeds, lime juice, agave nectar, chili pepper and mint and whisk well.

Pour this over salad, toss to coat well and serve cold.

Enjoy!

Nutrition: calories 89, fat 3, fiber 2, carbs 8, protein 2

Simple Radish Salad

It's a quick and simple salad you will definitely enjoy!

Preparation time: 10 minutes

Cooking time: 0 minutes

Servings: 4

Ingredients:

1 cup red onion, sliced
2 cusp radishes, sliced
1 garlic clove, minced
A pinch of salt and black pepper
2 tablespoons balsamic vinegar
1 cup cucumber, sliced
1 teaspoon dill, chopped
½ cup olive oil

Directions:

In a salad bowl, mix onion with cucumber, radishes, garlic, a pinch of salt and black pepper and stir.

Add vinegar, dill and oil, toss to coat and serve.

Enjoy!

Nutrition: calories 80, fat 1, fiber 2, carbs 5, protein 7

Delicious Okra Salad

This is crunchy and fresh!

Preparation time: 40 minutes
Cooking time: 0 minutes
Servings: 4
Ingredients:
1 pound okra, cut in medium pieces
A pinch of sea salt
Black pepper to the taste
15 ounces canned black beans, drained
1 cup corn
1 pound cherry tomatoes, halved
1 white onion, chopped
3 tablespoons olive oil
1 avocado, pitted, peeled and chopped

Directions:
Put okra in a salad bowl.
Add beans, corn, onion, tomatoes and avocado and stir.
Add a pinch of salt, black pepper and olive oil ,toss to coat and keep in the fridge for 30 minutes before you serve it.
Enjoy!

Nutrition: calories 120, fat 1, fiber 1, carbs 0, protein 7

Fresh Okra Salad

This is colored and super tasty salad idea!

Preparation time: 10 minutes

Cooking time: 0 minutes

Servings: 4

3 cups okra, chopped

1 big tomato, chopped

3 celery stalks, chopped

1 onion, chopped

3 cups cauliflower florets, chopped

1 yellow bell pepper, chopped

A pinch of sea salt

Black pepper to the taste

Juice from 1 lemon

½ teaspoon red pepper flakes

1 teaspoon garlic powder

Directions:

In a salad bowl, mix okra with tomato, celery stalks, onion, cauliflower and bell pepper.

Add a pinch of salt, black pepper, lemon juice, pepper flakes and garlic powder, toss to coat and serve.

Enjoy!

Nutrition: calories 80, fat 0, fiber 1, carbs 0, protein 5

Corn Salad

This is perfect for a hot day!

Preparation time: 10 minutes
Cooking time: 0 minutes
Servings: 4
Ingredients:
1 and ½ teaspoons agave nectar
2 tablespoons lime juice
1 jalapeno, chopped
¼ cup olive oil
¼ teaspoon cumin, ground
A pinch of sea salt
Black pepper to the taste
4 cups fresh corn kernels
½ cup parsley, chopped
6 radishes, thinly sliced
1 red onion, chopped
Directions:

In your blender, mix agave nectar with lime juice, jalapeno, cumin, oil, salt and pepper and blend well.

In a salad bowl, mix corn with onion, radishes and parsley.

Add salad dressing, toss to coat and serve.

Nutrition: calories 100, fat 0.4, fiber 0.8, carbs 1, protein 6

Corn And Arugula Salad

You have to make this salad tonight!

Preparation time: 10 minutes

Cooking time: 0 minutes

Servings: 4

Ingredients:

1 red bell pepper, thinly sliced

2 cups corn

Juice from 1 lemon

Zest from 1 lemon, grated

8 cups arugula

A pinch of sea salt

Black pepper to the taste

Directions:

In a salad bowl, mix arugula with corn and bell pepper.

Add salt, pepper, lemon zest and juice, toss to coat and serve. Enjoy!

Nutrition: calories 90, fat 0, fiber 1, carbs 1, protein 5

Corn and Bulgur Salad

This is not just very tasty! It's also very healthy!

Preparation time: 30 minutes
Cooking time: 0 minutes
Servings: 4
Ingredients:
1 cup bulgur
2 cups hot water
A pinch of sea salt
Black pepper to the taste
2 cups corn
1 cucumber, chopped
2 tablespoons lemon juice
2 tablespoons balsamic vinegar
¼ cup olive oil
Directions:

In a bowl, mix bulgur with the water, cover, leave aside for 25 minutes, fluff with a fork and transfer to a salad bowl.

Add corn and cucumber and stir.

In a small bowl, mix oil with lemon juice, vinegar, salt and pepper and whisk well.

Add this to your salad, toss to coat well and serve.

Nutrition: calories 100, fat 0.5, fiber 2, carbs 2, protein 6

Mini Bell Pepper Salad

This is full of amazing colors and delicious tastes!

Preparation time: 10 minutes

Cooking time: 0 minutes

Servings: 4

Ingredients:

2 tablespoons dill, chopped

1 sweet onion, chopped

1 pound multi colored bell peppers, cut in halves, seeded and cut in thin strips

3 tablespoons olive oil

2 and ½ tablespoons white vinegar

A pinch of sea salt

Black pepper to the taste

Directions:

In a salad bowl, mix bell peppers with onion and dill.

Add salt, pepper, oil and vinegar, toss to coat and serve.

Enjoy!

Nutrition: calories 80, fat 0, fiber 1, carbs 2, protein 3

Bell Pepper And Avocado Salad

This is great for lunch!

Preparation time: 10 minutes

Cooking time: 0 minutes

Servings: 1

Ingredients:

2 green onions, chopped

½ cup cherry tomatoes, halved

1 red bell pepper, chopped

2 tablespoons parsley, chopped

Juice from 1 lemon

Salt and black pepper to the taste

1 avocado, pitted, peeled and chopped

Directions:

In a salad bowl, mix tomatoes with onions, bell pepper, parsley, avocado, salt and pepper and stir.

Add lemon juice, toss well and serve.

Enjoy!

Nutrition: calories 67, fat 0, fiber 1, carbs 2, protein 6

Crispy Asparagus Salad

Have you ever tried a raw asparagus salad?

Preparation time: 15 minutes
Cooking time: 0 minutes
Servings: 4
Ingredients:
½ cup walnuts, chopped
1/3 cup breadcrumbs, dried
Salt and black pepper to the taste
1 teaspoon lemon zest, grated
A pinch of chili flakes, dried
¼ cup lemon juice
1 pound asparagus, trimmed and cut in medium pieces
¼ cup mint leaves
A drizzle of olive oil

Directions:

In a bowl, mix breadcrumbs with walnuts, lemon zest, salt, pepper and chili flakes and stir well.

In a salad bowl, mix asparagus with breadcrumbs mix, lemon juice, mint and oil, toss to coat well and serve.

Enjoy!

Nutrition: calories 100, fat 1, fiber 0, carbs 0, protein 6

Napa Cabbage And Peanut Dressing

It's creamy and really delicious!

Preparation time: 10 minutes
Cooking time: 0 minutes
Servings: 4
Ingredients:
½ cup red bell pepper, cut in thin strips
1 carrot, grated
4 cups napa cabbage, shredded
3 green onions, chopped
1 tablespoon rice syrup
1 tablespoon sesame oil
2 teaspoons ginger, grated
½ teaspoon red pepper flakes, crushed
3 tablespoons rice vinegar
1 tablespoon soy sauce
3 tablespoons vegan peanut butter

Directions:

In a salad bowl, mix bell pepper with carrot, cabbage and onions and toss.

In another bowl, mix rice syrup with oil, ginger, pepper flakes, vinegar, soy sauce and peanut butter and whisk really well.

Add this to salad, toss to coat well and serve.

Enjoy!

Nutrition: calories 160, fat 10, fiber 3, carbs 10, protein 5

Tasty Napa Cabbage Salad And Almonds

It's full of amazing taste and flavor!

Preparation time: 10 minutes

Cooking time: 0 minutes

Servings: 4

Ingredients:

1 napa cabbage, shredded

1 cup almonds, chopped

1 bunch green onions, chopped

¼ cup blueberries, dried

¼ cup rice vinegar

2 tablespoons soy sauce

½ cup olive oil

¼ teaspoon ginger, grated

A pinch of black pepper

Directions:

In a salad bowl, mix almonds with cabbage, onions and blueberries.

In another bowl, mix vinegar with soy sauce, oil, black pepper and ginger and whisk well.

Add this to your salad, toss to coat and serve.

Enjoy!

Nutrition: calories 140, fat 3, fiber 3, carbs 8, protein 6

Tasty Napa Cabbage Salad And Tamari Dressing

You really need to learn how to make this wonderful salad!

Preparation time: 10 minutes
Cooking time: 0 minutes
Servings: 4
Ingredients:
7 scallions, chopped
1 napa cabbage head, shredded
1 red bell pepper, halved and cut in thin strips
2 carrots, chopped
½ cup cilantro, chopped
3 tablespoons sunflower seeds
2 tablespoons sesame seeds
¼ cup rice vinegar
1 tablespoon sesame oil
3 and ½ tablespoons olive oil
1 tablespoon tamari sauce
1 tablespoon maple syrup

Directions:

In a salad bowl, mix cabbage with scallions, bell pepper, carrots and cilantro and stir.

In another bowl, mix vinegar with sesame oil, olive oil, tamari sauce and maple syrup and whisk well.

Pour this over salad, toss to coat and serve with sunflower and sesame seeds on top.

Enjoy!

Nutrition: calories 140, fat 4, fiber 3, carbs 5, protein 6

Simple Celery Salad

Serve this for dinner tonight!

Preparation time: 10 minutes

Cooking time: 0 minutes

Servings: 4

Ingredients:

½ cup raisins

4 cups celery, sliced

¼ cup parsley, chopped

½ cup walnuts, chopped

Juice from ½ lemon

2 tablespoons olive oil

Salt and black pepper to the taste

Directions:

In a salad bowl, mix celery with raisins, walnuts and parsley and stir.

Add lemon juice, oil, salt and pepper, toss to coat and serve right away. Enjoy!

Nutrition: calories 120, fat 1, fiber 2, carbs 3, protein 5

Healthy Celery Salad

This is so healthy and easy to make! You should try it soon!

Preparation time: 10 minutes

Cooking time: 0 minutes

Servings: 4

Ingredients:

5 teaspoons macadamia honey

½ cup lemon juice

1/3 cup Dijon mustard

2/3 cup olive oil

Black pepper to the taste

A pinch of smoked sea salt

2 apples, cored, peeled and cut in medium cubes

1 bunch celery and leaves, roughly chopped

¾ cup walnuts, chopped

Directions:

In a salad bowl, mix celery and its leaves with apple pieces and walnuts.

Add salt and pepper and toss well.

In another bowl, mix lemon juice with mustard, macadamia honey and olive oil and whisk well.

Add this to salad, toss to coat and serve.

Nutrition: calories 100, fat 2, fiber 2, carbs 4, protein 7

Pomegranate And Celery Salad

It's so amazing and colored!

Preparation time: 10 minutes

Cooking time: 0 minutes

Servings: 4

Ingredients:

6 celery stalks, chopped and leaves reserved

1 garlic clove, minced

¼ cup olive oil

3 tablespoons balsamic vinegar

Salt and black pepper to the taste

1 teaspoon allspice, ground

½ cup parsley, chopped

2 pomegranates, arils removed

Directions:

In a bowl, mix celery with garlic, salt, pepper, oil and allspice.

Stir, add parsley and pomegranate arils and serve.

Enjoy!

Nutrition: calories 90, fat 2, fiber 1, carbs 1, protein 5

Grated Cauliflower Salad

We are sure you've never tried something like this before!

Preparation time: 10 minutes
Cooking time: 0 minutes
Servings: 4
Ingredients:
½ carrot, grated
½ cup red bell pepper, chopped
½ cup zucchini, chopped
3 cups cauliflower, grated
¼ cup parsley, chopped
For the salad dressing:
1 teaspoon ginger, grated
1 tablespoon olive oil
1 tablespoon lime juice
2 teaspoons agave nectar
1 teaspoon jalapeno, minced
A pinch of sea salt
Black pepper to the taste

Directions:

In a salad bowl, mix cauliflower with carrot, bell pepper, zucchini and parsley and stir.

In another bowl, mix oil with lime juice, agave nectar, ginger, jalapeno, salt and pepper and whisk well.

Add this to your salad, toss to coat and serve cold.

Enjoy!

Nutrition: calories 100, fat 1, fiber 4, carbs 10, protein 3

Cauliflower Salad And Mustard Vinaigrette

The combination is pretty awesome!

Preparation time: 10 minutes
Cooking time: 0 minutes
Servings: 4
Ingredients:
1 cup cucumber, sliced
1 cup tomatoes, chopped
1 cauliflower head, florets chopped
¼ cup spring onion, chopped
For the salad dressing:
1 date, chopped
½ cup water
½ cup cashews, soaked and drained
2 tablespoons coconut aminos
1 teaspoon mustard powder
2 tablespoons dill, chopped
2 garlic cloves, minced
Zest and juice from ½ lemon
Salt and black pepper to the taste
½ cup walnuts, chopped

Directions:
In your blender, mix cashews with water, date, mustard powder and coconut aminos and blend well.

Add dill, lemon zest and juice, garlic, walnuts, salt and pepper, blend again well and leave aside for now.

In a salad bowl, mix cauliflower with cucumber, tomato and onion and stir.

Add salad dressing you've made earlier and serve.

Enjoy!

Nutrition: calories 120, fat 2, fiber 2, carbs 3, protein 6

Green Beans Salad

It's a savory salad you will enjoy for sure!

Preparation time: 10 minutes
Cooking time: 0 minutes
Servings: 4
Ingredients:
8 ounces green beans, sliced
1 cup cherry tomatoes, halved
1 garlic clove, minced
6 basil leaves, chopped
A pinch of red pepper flakes, crushed
A pinch of sea salt
For the salad dressing:
¼ cup balsamic vinegar
¾ cup olive oil
2 tablespoons white vinegar
Directions:
In a salad bowl, mix green beans with cherry tomatoes, basil, garlic, pepper flakes and some salt and stir.

Add white vinegar, balsamic vinegar and oil and toss to coat.

Serve right away.

Enjoy!

Nutrition: calories 100, fat 2, fiber 2, carbs 4, protein 6

Spring Green Beans Salad

This spring salad is very fresh and tasty!

Preparation time: 10 minutes

Cooking time: 0 minutes

Servings: 6

Ingredients:

1 big cucumber, sliced

1 pound green beans, halved

1 red chili pepper, chopped

1 garlic clove, minced

1 tablespoon agave nectar

¼ cup lime juice

A pinch of sea salt

¼ cup canola oil

Directions:

In a salad bowl, mix cucumber with green beans, chili and garlic and stir. Add lime juice, salt, agave nectar and oil, toss to coat well and serve. Enjoy!

Nutrition: calories 100, fat 1, fiber 2, carbs 2, protein 6

Delicious Green Beans And Leeks Salad

You should consider trying this tasty combination right away!

Preparation time: 20 minutes

Cooking time: 0 minutes

Servings: 4

Ingredients:

2 cups green beans, sliced

1 cup carrot, shredded

2 tablespoons olive oil

1 and ½ teaspoons ginger, grated

2 tablespoons leek, chopped

A pinch of sea salt

2 teaspoons unpasteurized soy sauce

½ teaspoon cumin, ground

½ teaspoon coriander, ground

½ teaspoon curry powder

½ teaspoon garam masala

1 teaspoon lime juice

1 tablespoon agave nectar

Directions:

In a salad bowl, mix green beans with carrots, leeks, ginger, salt, oil and soy sauce and toss well.

Add cumin, coriander, curry powder, garam masala, agave nectar and lime juice, toss well again and serve.

Enjoy!

Nutrition: calories 120, fat 3, fiber 4, carbs 6, protein 6

Wonderful Green Beans Salad

This is easy to make and you can enjoy it both for lunch or dinner!

Preparation time: 10 minutes

Cooking time: 0 minutes

Servings: 4

Ingredients:

2 cups green beans, cut in medium pieces

1 red onion, chopped

2 cups cherry tomatoes, halved

2 garlic cloves, minced

3 tablespoons olive oil

Juice from 1 lemon

1 teaspoon rosemary, chopped

1 teaspoon thyme, chopped

A pinch of salt

Directions:

In a salad bowl, mix green beans with onion and tomatoes.

In another bowl, mix lemon juice with oil, garlic, thyme, rosemary and salt and whisk well.

Add this to your salad, toss to coat and serve.

Enjoy!

Nutrition: calories 100, fat 1, fiber 2, carbs 3, protein 5

Cauliflower And Green Beans Salad

It's an amazing salad you can serve with a tasty pesto!

Preparation time: 10 minutes
Cooking time: 0 minutes
Servings: 4
Ingredients:
1 pound green beans, chopped
1 tomato, chopped
½ cup pecans, chopped
Salt and black pepper to the taste
½ cauliflower head, chopped
For the pesto:
¼ cup olive oil
2 cups basil leaves
1 garlic clove, minced
1 tablespoon lemon juice
Directions:

In your blender, mix basil with oil, garlic and lemon juice, pulse really well and leave aside for now.

In a salad bowl, mix green beans with cauliflower, tomato, pecans, salt and pepper and stir.

Add pesto, toss to coat well and serve.

Nutrition: calories 100, fat 2, fiber 2, carbs 3, protein 6

Tasty Leeks Salad

You only need a few ingredients to make a tasty salad!

Preparation time: 5 minutes

Cooking time: 0 minutes

Servings: 3

Ingredients:

Juice from ½ lemon

2 leeks, sliced

½ teaspoon oregano, dried

2 tablespoons olive oil

A pinch of sea salt

Black pepper to the taste

Directions:

In a salad bowl, mix leeks with oregano, a pinch of salt and black pepper and stir.

Add oil and lemon juice, toss well and serve.

Enjoy!

Nutrition: calories 70, fat 0, fiber 1, carbs 1, protein 5

Unbelievable Leeks Salad

It's unbelievably tasty!

Preparation time: 15 minutes
Cooking time: 0 minutes
Servings: 4
Ingredients:
1 bunch radishes, sliced
3 cups leeks, chopped
1 and ½ cups olives, pitted and sliced
A pinch of turmeric
A pinch of sea salt
Black pepper to the taste
2 tablespoons olive oil
1 cup cilantro, chopped
½ avocado, pitted, peeled and cubed

Directions:

In a salad bowl, mix radishes with leeks, olives, cilantro and avocado cubes and toss.

Add salt, pepper, oil and turmeric, toss to coat and leave aside for 15 minutes before serving.

Enjoy!

Nutrition: calories 100, fat 1, fiber 1, carbs 3, protein 6

Incredible Brussels Sprouts Salad

It's a summer salad even your kids will love!

Preparation time: 10 minutes

Cooking time: 0 minutes

Servings: 10

Ingredients:

24 ounces Brussels sprouts, shredded

1 cup red onion, chopped

2/3 cup cherries, dried

2/3 cup almonds, chopped

For the vinaigrette:

Juice from 1 lemon

1 teaspoon orange zest

Juice from 1 orange

2 tablespoons shallots, chopped

1 teaspoon mustard

2/3 cup avocado oil

Salt and black pepper to the taste

2 teaspoons thyme, chopped

Directions:

In a bowl, combine lemon juice with orange juice, orange zest, shallots, mustard, oil, salt, pepper and thyme and whisk really well.

In a salad bowl, mix Brussels sprouts with almonds, cherries and onion and stir.

Add the vinaigrette you've made, toss well and serve.

Enjoy!

Nutrition: calories 100, fat 1, fiber 1, carbs 2, protein 5

Brussels Sprouts And Apples Salad

This delightful salad is actually pretty easy to make at home!

Preparation time: 35 minutes

Cooking time: 0 minutes

Servings: 6

Ingredients:

1 pound Brussels sprouts, shredded

1 cup walnuts, chopped

1 apple, cored and cubed

1 red onion, chopped

For the salad dressing:

3 tablespoons red vinegar

1 tablespoon mustard

2 teaspoons maple syrup

½ cup olive oil

1 garlic clove, minced

A pinch of sea salt

Black pepper to the taste

Directions:

In a salad bowl, mix sprouts with apple, onion and walnuts and stir.

In another bowl, mix vinegar with mustard, maple syrup, oil, garlic, salt and pepper and whisk really well.

Add this to your salad, toss well and serve.

Enjoy!

Nutrition: calories 100, fat 2, fiber 2, carbs 2, protein 1

Tasty Mung Sprouts Salad

If you are looking for a really delicious dinner idea, then why don't you try this next salad?

Preparation time: 10 minutes

Cooking time: 0 minutes

Servings: 2

Ingredients:

1 red onion, chopped

2 cups mung beans, sprouted

A pinch of red chili powder

1 green chili pepper, chopped

1 tomato, chopped

1 teaspoon chaat masala

1 teaspoon lemon juice

1 tablespoon coriander, chopped

Lemon slices for serving

A pinch of sea salt

Black pepper to the taste

Directions:

In a salad bowl, mix onion with mung sprouts, chili pepper and tomato.

Add red chili powder, chaat masala, lemon juice, coriander, salt and pepper and toss well.

Serve with lemon slices on the side.

Enjoy!

Nutrition: calories 100, fat 2, fiber 1, carbs 3, protein 6

Delicious Mung Beans Salad

We love this salad and we think you will appreciate it too!

Preparation time: 10 minutes

Cooking time: 0 minutes

Servings: 6

Ingredients:

2 cups tomatoes, chopped

2 cups cucumber, chopped

3 cups mixed greens

2 cups mung beans, sprouted

2 cups clover sprouts

For the salad dressing:

1 tablespoon cumin, ground

1 cup dill, chopped

4 tablespoons lemon juice

1 avocado, pitted, peeled and roughly chopped

1 cucumber, roughly chopped

Directions:

In a salad bowl, mix tomatoes with 2 cups cucumber, greens, clover and mung sprouts and stir.

In your blender, mix cumin with dill, lemon juice, 1 cucumber and avocado and blend really well.

Add this to your salad, toss well and serve.

Enjoy!

Nutrition: calories 80, fat 0, fiber 0.5, carbs 1, protein 6

Conclusion

This wonderful cooking journal is going to change your life for ever! It's the only cookbook available on the market written in a catching and unique manner that can attract readers!

This ultimate vegan salads cookbook is going to become your new best friend in the kitchen!

It will teach you how to make some of the most amazing, delicious, colored and textured vegan salads!

How does this sound?

So, don't wait too long! Gather your ingredients and make some of the best vegan salads in the world!

Have fun!

Author's Note

Thank you for downloading this book!

Did you enjoy Raw Vegan Salads: 60 The most delicious recipes? Have you created any of these simple salads at home? I hope this book was able to help you to prepare delicious raw vegan salads.

Finally, if you liked this book and would like to help other people to change their lives, please consider leaving a short review on Amazon. Please share the book link with your friends and help them to improve health with the help of proper nutrition. It'd be greatly appreciated!

Thank You!

Be healthy and happy every day!

Best Wishes,
Maya Fedichi

Printed in Great Britain
by Amazon